The Man Who Can Look Backward

THE MAN WHO CAN LOOK BACKWARD

NOEL STREET

Tarnhelm Press
Lakemont, Georgia 30552

Copyright © 1969
by Noel Street

First printing 1969—2000
Second printing 1971—2000
Third printing 1972—1500

Standard Book Number 0-87707-112-8

Printed for the publishers in the United States of
America by CSA Printing and Bindery, Inc.

ACKNOWLEDGEMENTS

It has only been possible to produce this book, which attempts to knit the past into the present, with the help of many other people.

Some of these have been the main actors in the experiences which make up the theme of the manuscript.

It would not be complete, however, without paying special tribute to the help given by the educated pen of Doris Herzog, one-time Hollywood journalist and now director of the Philosophical Research Center in New York. Both she, and her associate, Nesta Kerin Crain, have added encouragement and the wisdom of many years experience in the field of spiritual research.

The cover design was created by our friend Anne Riegel of Greenwich Village, who contributed her beauty of thought to that of the mature mind of the publisher, with whom she cooperated.

So, good friends all - thank you.

N. S.

THE MAN WHO CAN LOOK BACKWARD
CHAPTER SUMMARY

FOREWORD   9

(1) **REINCARNATION** - We are all Citizens of Eternity. Historical facts about re-birth, its place in Christianity. Our past lives are all recorded. How they affect us today. Release of blockages. How my career began in this field.   11

(2) **LINKS OR ATTACHMENTS FROM EARLIER LIVES** - How our past encounters can be repeated Psychic attachments. Magnetism and sex powers. Magic and sorcery in Washington D.C. Time intervals between incarnations. Old souls - new souls; twin-souls, soul-mates. Your spiritual-name. Special re-associations. Nothing accidental ever happens to us. How we attain spiritual joy.   18

(3) **IS IT BENEFICIAL TO KNOW ABOUT YOUR PREVIOUS LIVES?** - Why the interest? History repeats itself again and again. Mankind's great search. The law of Karma. The Great Ones' profound simplicities. The Divine Light. Hindu greeting. "One life - many births." People's reasons for wanting to know their past. The Queen of Sheba nearly returns in New York. Perfumed records.   27

(4) **WHAT IS THE PURPOSE OF REINCARNATION?** Apparent inequalities of birth - why? How we progress. The Psalmist and the immutable law. The Bhagavad-Gita, Revelation. Our spiritual power and how to increase it. The steps to the Christhood. Reactions of people who have never heard of Christ. Older souls now coming back for a special purpose.   34

(5) **HOW IS RE-BIRTH POSSIBLE?** - What is the soul? What happens when we die? The modus operandi of reincarnation. Our Mother-Spirit. Our instincts. Man's links with the sub-conscious and the God-head. Transmigration of souls. Group souls. The London gynaecologist. The Lords of Karma. The spirit-"bank", soul-rays - their colors and growth.   40

(6) **VERIFIABLE EVIDENCE OF FORMER EARTH-LIVES** - Truth seekers; need for neutrality. Many well-authenticated Indian "recalls." My own reincarnation-week with three remarkable happenings. L. T. Symons - Astralian psychic extraordinary. Old Inca priest returns. The Czech warrior-of-old. The bookshop keeper in New Zealand. An old song comes back. French Revolution recall. Playing a spinet. Afghan hounds. "You were my wife" says the Indian body. 47

(7) **MAN'S IMMORTAL HERITAGE** - Life and death; Taking life. Churchill, Hitler, God. New Jersey paper reports on a recent meeting; the sequel. A sixty-four page letter. New educational outlook on religion in American Universities. Changing freedoms of thought. Less dogma more participation. Readers write from all over the world. 56

(8) **HOW YOUR LIFE CAN AFFECT THE WHOLE WORLD** - Religious inaccuracies. Fossils. Extinct civilizations. "Built by unknown hands" Indonesia. Life on other planets. Pilgrim-gods. By their fruits ye shall know them. Knowing truth direct, not second-hand. How to be sure. The sign of the cross. 66

(9) **SPIRITUAL VISIBILITY BECOMING CLEARER** Man's "last-enemy" analyzed. Becoming free of all fear. Life's continuous river. An Aztec flash-back. Do animals reincarnate? Readers, please write. Satan speaks. How we make our own progress. Miracles. 73

(10) **THE KEY TO YOUR SPIRITUAL TREASURE HOUSE** - Your motive determines your progress. Light and meditation. A way into the Silence explained in detail. Its use by individuals and groups. Attainment of of the Spirit of Truth. 79

(11) **CONCLUSION** - We carve our destiny or dig our grave. How do we all end - Satan, Judas? The eternal library holds all truth - interesting evidence. How to become a member. Riding the pathway to reincarnation. 86

FOREWORD

Noel Street's path has led to many Greats of the Wisdom Life who serve where the directive leads them. From London, he moved through Egypt and parts of the Near East, India on to Australia and New Zealand where his Spiritual Center was established and opened to all seeking a Healer, a Reincarnation Consultant and a Teacher of Spiritual Development and Meditation.

His recent move has brought him and his wife Colleen - also a Spiritual server whose interests are largely in improving the individual's health through teaching Hatha Yoga - - to the United States. Here, through appearing on television, the radio and speaking and teaching throughout the country he has become widely known and deeply appreciated.

The writer of this Foreword and her associate, Nesta Kerin Crain, became happily linked with Noel and Colleen Street through a friend of our Philosophical Research Center in New York city, a center that has known many in this Work since its birth in April, 1941. The friend, Mrs. Aileen Bourné, telephoned to tell us about one Noel Street of New Zealand who had written her and asked if she could recommend anyone who might be interested in his work. It was sometime later that she was awakened in the middle of the night out of a sound sleep by a Voice instructing her to tell Philosophical Research about Noel Street. She did and since the Spring of 1968 this Center has welcomed Noel Street, hundreds have come to his lectures and attended his classes. Many have received depthful understanding through his guidance and now walk in understanding in the Light.

In the times of spiritual darkness and suffering and great need, the Ancient Sages teach that great Souls are sent into the world - into the valley of men - with the Light. Noel Street is of those who so Serve, dedicated to the Eleventh Commandment given by the Man of Peace: "A new commandment I give unto you - Love one another."

Love - spelt in reverse - is evol(ve). Through evolving into Spiritual enlightenment Love reveals Itself - a great peace is re-born in man's heart - and the shadows are embraced by the Light.

This is of Noel Street's work. Read on now to his words as "The Man Who Can Look Backward" and may you be blessed with the Light he shares in this incursion into Reincarnation wherein the Past is the Parent of the Present, and the Present, of the Future.

Doris Herzog

1

THE MAN WHO CAN LOOK BACKWARD......

Reincarnation

"Your Passport... sir ... please," A routine enquiry, evoking no particular reaction in the normal way, repeated probably thousands of times in various languages every day of the year.

Followed by, "Your Passport ... sir ... thank you." With no particular emotion the booklet is returned, perhaps stamped, to be replaced in a pocket or briefcase, ready for further inspection when required.

This shows where you have been, or perhaps intend to go, on your travels in this present life. A record of your journeys from one place to another, some of which you would like to re-visit if opportunity permitted.

This same question, phrased in exactly the same manner, however, did cause many hearts to beat in desperate fear and anxiety about twenty-five years ago when frontier-guards were on the look-out for illegal entrants in many parts of the world.

A year or two ago I was lecturing to a Yoga school in Melbourne when I noticed several numbers on the wrist of one woman. The blue-black ink indelibly stamped on her body reflected to my eyes the reason for the anguish lurking in hers. Her black leotard could be removed but this concentration-camp's seal represented one place where she would never like to return.

Do you believe the eyes are the mirror of the soul? I do.

Whether we like it or not, we are all Citizens of Eternity and as most of us have lived on this old Mother Earth many times in various guises we therefore possess eternal passports.

Although man's viewpoint may differ as to whether we occupy more than one physical body on earth, all religious teachings show that life continues after death and some people may find it difficult to fit in the idea of reincarnation with their particular spiritual tenets.

Had that same person been born in India instead of possibly an English-speaking country it would have been equally difficult not to believe in re-birth as some 250 million Hindus and 150 million Buddhists are brought-up with an understanding of this belief, which briefly means that our spirit is continuous and requires more than one physical life to attain to a state of purity.

Most of us, as we pass through life, whether believing in re-birth, or not, have questioned the obvious inequalities of birth of the various races of the world. Some appear to be much better placed than others. We often meet people, too, who tell us they remember having been in a place before, or perhaps having met someone before. Most of us question the fairness of the Creator who allows little mongol or cretin children to incarnate unless this be part of a definite plan, rather than a chance-of-birth.

Have you ever considered why it is you have

Reincarnation

certain likings for whole races of people, or perhaps feel definite affinities with certain specific religions?

If you have lived happily in such races in earlier lifetimes, or worshipped joyously in such religions, you would have an answer to each question.

Conversely, of course, the opposite applies. We all know persons who are quite happy to say they dislike "Indians," "Scotsmen" or "Jewish" people for no apparent reason. Also some people have a very positive dislike when meeting a particular person for the first time. These strange reactions are difficult to explain without an understanding of reincarnation.

There are many attested cases of child-prodigies in various fields. Their physical lineage does not explain their exceptional talents and it is in such instances that we find especially interesting such statements as those attributed to Plato that, "Knowledge which flows back easily is that which has been gained in previous lives," or to Confucious, "Some men are born wise, others learn by toil."

It is difficult to pinpoint historically when the concept of re-birth first appeared. References in ancient Sanskrit writings appear to relate to reincarnation. A beautiful passage appears in the Egyptian Book of the Dead, written by unknown hands, thousands of years ago: "Infinite time, without beginning and without end, hath been given to me; I inherit eternity and everlastingness hath been bestowed upon me." The phrase, "Thou art old, O my soul; yea thou art from everlasting," is taken from one of the Hermetic works, which may be even older than the Book of the Dead.

Reincarnation was originally a Christian teaching and several of Jesus' references to John-the-Baptist confirm that He believed John to be a reincarnation of the spirit of Elijah. Also, Jesus seems to have referred to it as though it were part of the accepted ideas of His day. He never taught that it was false nor did He repudiate or deny it. When speaking of John-the-Baptist in Matthew II, He said, "This is Elijah which is to come," and in the 17th chapter of this gospel, verses 11-13, is confirmation that He believed John-the-Baptist to be a reincarnation of Elijah.

In this reference it is interesting to read the penultimate verse of the Old Testament, "Behold I will send you Elijah the prophet before the coming of the great and dreadful day of the Lord." Some historians consider this may have been written four hundred years B.C., if not earlier.

That His disciples were familiar with the belief is obvious from chap. 16 of St. Matthew when Jesus said, "Whom do men say that I the Son of man am?" And the Disciple answered, "Some say that thou art John-the-Baptist: some, Elias; and others, Jeremias, or one of the prophets." The early Church appears to have become disenchanted with the teacher Origen who emphasized pre-existence and condemned him for his beliefs at the Council of Constantinople, A.D. 553 by three votes to two. From that time reincarnation seems to have lost favor in general Christian teachings although many brave thinkers continued to teach their belief in reincarnation including St. Augustine and St. Francis-of-Assisi.

In just the same way as the tremendous impact made on the psyche of the Yoga student in Australia, who spent some years in a concentration-camp, so these spiritual teachers had doubtless - in earlier earth-lives - been familiar with reincarnation and, as Plato said, "the knowledge flows back easily."

People may ask, "Why can't I remember my past lives?" The Buddha - we are told - stated that he had had many earlier lives and "all of them I know." We are aware of the illumined state of the Buddha's mind and of his attainment of cosmic-consciousness;

Reincarnation

therefore to him, it was a relatively easy task to recall his former lives, as there were no blocks or obstacles in the way. Homo sapiens finds it difficult to remember even a movie which he might have seen only a few months ago. But he blames the movie. It was so poor it didn't register. However, after some concentration he can generally recall a few incidents from the film and should he see it again it is probable he will feel it was only last night that he last saw it.

And so it is with our past lives. They are all recorded. As you read further you will find there are many people with an awareness, which amounts to a definite challenge to their lives today, of their past soulic-history.

Sometimes our illnesses or the disappointments in our life are simply carry-overs from earlier experiences on earth.

In 1959 an elderly lady was consulting me in my Clinic in London. Her illness was most distressing to her in that she could not go out in crowds of people without having someone with her. This was indeed a great difficulty in London. I tried to help her with standard techniques. During one of these meetings in a very serious voice, she enquired: "Do you think, Reverend Street, this condition could be a carry-over from an earlier life?" While I was deeply interested in Reincarnation, I did not know then that it was possible for me to see "backwards" in time, even as the Buddha had over his own earlier lives. I certainly knew of a few who had this "seeing" gift, but not in such a way as to be able to influence the present life. In other words, it was more theory than knowledge that not only do our earlier earth-lives condition our present one, but each incarnation enables us to overcome weaknesses and remove their influence.

I have always had a profound faith in the power of Spirit never to let one down in times of need, so

THE MAN WHO CAN LOOK BACKWARD

I prayed very hard that I might be used to help this poor woman. Suddenly out of nowhere appeared scenes before my consciousness. I described them to her. In one, she was excited to recognize "herself" in a seething crowd-scene at the Roman games where many were crushed to death. The cause of her fear of crowds now identified, I was able, through the use of a healing technique, to reach her Christ-consciousness and free her from this fear.

After this happening, people commenced to make appointments to see me, not necessarily because they were ill but to verify certain flash-memories of past-lives and often to seek confirmation that their present spiritual pathway was correct. In this manner my life as a Reincarnation Consultant began.

I was invited by various groups and societies to lecture on the subject and I was always asked if I could give a demonstration of tracing past lives of members of the audience. At first, this was extremely difficult as the consciousness must be in a most acute state as the records of people's past earth lives are shown. Every sound is magnified and the demonstrations would often be interrupted by disgruntled people stomping out when they found they had not been chosen as a subject.

However, I demonstrated to more and more public groups, regardless of the unbelievers and the sceptics. This was more satisfying to me personally as I was able to combine this with my own spiritual healing activities and thus follow the Biblical instructions to spread the word and heal the sick.

I believe I am the only man to have ever demonstrated this faculty on television and I have now visited many countries in my spiritual service, including India, Indonesia, Australia, Egypt, France, England, the United States and New Zealand where I lived for a number of years. In 1968 I was appearing in public

Reincarnation

demonstrations of both psychic healing and reincarnation readings in many American cities including New York, Chicago, Cincinnati, Washington D.C., and other cities in California, Florida and Georgia.

Of course, it is easier now for me to do these reincarnation readings as I know better what to expect when I go into "the Silence." Everybody has a spiritual name, or permanent name by which they are known in the heavens. The present earth-name provides the necessary link with the spiritual name to which all the past records are attached and such aspects as are pertinent to a reading are shown. I find it equally easy to do this type of work by mail as in person. I need a photograph of the person for whom I read. It must show his eyes. These particular readings have given, and do give, much comfort and help to many people in sometimes very remote parts of the world.

. . . .

"I hold that when a person dies,
His soul returns again to earth;
Arrayed in some new flesh-disguise
Another mother gives him birth.
With sturdier limbs and brighter brain
The old soul takes the road again."

English Poet Laureate John Masefield

2

LINKS OR ATTACHMENTS FROM EARLIER LIVES

Even as it is relatively common to meet a person you feel a strong affinity to and that you may have known before, it is also of interest to find the exact opposite happening. It surprised me once to see two young children, both of whom were loving and natural to everyone else, meet for the first time, stop dead in their tracks and just feel hatred for the other. Strange, isn't it? Yet, in the light of their having known each other in bitter conditions in an earlier life, it is not hard to understand.

From my readings of people's past-lives I have found other attachments, sometimes of a quite dramatic nature, are still very much live, although the original bondage may have been established thousands of years ago. This seems to be particularly applicable to when magnetism is used by one person to gain control over others. This magnetism can be embedded in soul-links, sex-ties, psychic control or in other ways in which spiritual power is used to influence and dominate another's will.

Links or Attachments From Earlier Lives

True spiritual power is born through love for humanity and Nature's kingdoms. A saint has been described as one whose love embraces all. It is the ultimate mission of every person to reach in understanding and in living the 11th commandment, "Love one another."

It is the ultimate necessity and spiritual responsibility of every person to realize in illumined consciousness the beauty of Love as indicated in this commandment, "Love one another."

But this is a different love than the physical. It includes the physical, of course, but its scintillating power carries to the very gates of Heaven. Before this illumination is achieved, as the cycles of time show through history - there are many tests, many pitfalls, much dismal failure and a lonely few but glorious successes. These negatives, however, have their silver lining. What dark cloud hasn't? Our Creator made both light and darkness, both positive and negative and within the pattern of the individual life, each through free will, determines which he will use. Therefore, each decides the course of his destiny, step by step, day by day. Every decision is a cause; every cause sets in motion effects. In terms of the religioscience of the Wisdom Schools, this keys us to Life and Lives ... motivated by our experiences, by our actions and reactions.

During a reading recently in the U.S. I found my visitor had been involved in an earlier life with a priest. Both in that life led celibate lives and both influenced the other to break their vows. As she was a nun, this decision was as disturbing to her as to him, but together they made a pact that they would be united through sex at all times. It is not difficult to do this, but it is very difficult to break such a pact once it has been made. Through several succeeding lives this soul was still influenced by extreme sex power, power she had apparently used to her own advantage. She was still using it in her present life and this she admitted she was doing, but now she wanted to know how to break this strange force influencing and shadowing her life.

To accomplish this, she had to break the force at its source and this was with her lover-priest of long ago, whose spirit was still linked with hers. I was able to show her how to do this.

One of the strangest links ever forged was still able to adversely influence a man who lived in Washington D.C. He did not speak much of his feelings to me as I went back along his life-track in various countries, until we found the difficulty. This originated in Egypt in the fifteen hundred year B.C time period. In this incarnation, when under hypnosis, his mind was "bonded" with another person who was dying. This was done by a magician. The magician had been able to control the dying man's mind. He still desired to do so. This dual-personality persisted through time and resulted in his being strangely affected in his present life whenever he heard the sound of cloth or paper being torn. This sound, no matter where he heard it, made his mind "go blank" and, he described his reaction as "someone influencing me."

In my work as a reincarnation reader and psychic healer I have met many who suffer from the influence of black magic, both from their past lives and current life. I have been able to help such unfortunates in their own efforts to free themselves from such bondage, for that is exactly what it is. It relates to magnetism and is immensely powerful - in some instances, terrifyingly so, for the force is invisible, though manifesting, and ignorance of the invisible can be a breeder of terror and anguish. It is the task of every genuine seeker on the path to become free of this influence, otherwise he will not progress very far. It is easy to

Links or Attachments From Earlier Lives

use but once set in motion, hard to break. But break it one must if one seeks to win through to the kingdom.

We know that we are instructed to love God with all our heart, all our mind and all our soul. But this is not possible if we are magnetically tied to another person. We can still love in a physical or mental sense, even if influenced by an outside force, but not spiritually. Love is the only real power we need to progress on the path. To gain this unity with God, in many cases we are forced to prove our worthiness by breaking some tie, either with another person or maybe a control imposed by a group of persons with whom we have been associated psychically.

It is often a near tragic and even a tragic business to free oneself of some magnetic attachment with another person, but once having broken such a bond the release and joy is stupendous.

I appreciate the layman may want to know how can this be proved. Perhaps the best answer is the old saying: "The proof of the pudding is in the eating." The proof of ALL TRUTH is in the realization and each receives according to how he seeks to conquer his problems and the "mutables" of these problems and how he strives to help those also seeking help.

There is no simple solution until we learn to understand the nuances and depths of our problems, and the more subtle and intangible their cause(s), the more difficult the answers. But there need be no reason for true seeker to despair. The promise has been made - and is always kept: "ask and it shall be given to you - knock and it shall open to you." And in this rhythm does the reader of reincarnations and psychic healing move in endeavoring to follow in the footsteps of the Master.

. . . .

THE MAN WHO CAN LOOK BACKWARD

I am often asked if we are attached to our present families as a result of earlier lives. As many readers will know, it is quite possible to keep in touch with our loved ones after they have passed into spirit. This can be done by the individual himself, provided he has developed this faculty, or - as is more generally done - through a medium, or channel who acts as a mediator between the visible and invisible worlds. It is fairly easy to establish this evidence and even to go back into several preceding generations, perhaps to our great grandparents, but there is very little, if any, evidence that spirits keep in touch with their families on earth for longer periods than, say, for one hundred years. What happens to that spirit who was perhaps your great grandmother? Has this spirit "gone on" in the spirit-world, or incarnated again in another physical body?

There is no pat rule as to the time interval between earth lives. This depends on the situation afforded by each birth, but many families have a feeling that they have known each other before, either as individuals or as a family group. This may well be, but the only link or attachment of any real value to us is that of love. Unselfish, kindly and the same love which the Master taught us to have one towards another. No doubt, our Creator in His great understanding does permit re-associations, but as with happy marriages, we can be quite sure they are the result of our having earned this great privilege. Let us say these physical reunions are an exception rather than the general rule.

There are, of course, old-souls and new-souls. The older variety are very distinct, being both supremely wise and very loving. Often having little in the way of possessions they have many friends. They may call you "dear....." with an ease of sincerity, whereas the younger souls are generally wanting to prove every- ting for their mind's sake. Often these eager ones have thin pointed noses - perhaps to be able to peer better at things - and try to rationalize matters of the spirit. It is generally a waste of time talking to them about spiritual subjects. They just are not ready. They are prone to use the word "practical" to describe their attitude to life. This not only implies but actually commits the person to material affairs. They will argue about religious topics and thoughts for hours on end and believe they speak with authority. They do - their own.

An old soul will not be drawn into argument on spiritual truths which he intuitively knows to be valid. He will reply to questions, if asked, but he won't argue. It is quite fascinating when one perceives an old soul in a child's body. Their answers are so unexpected. When one of my daughters was four years old, we had visited their grandmother in England. We were returning to London by car when she exclaimed:

"Granma's mad, Dad,"

"Why?" I asked defensively.

"Because she says pigs are her favorite animals, but she eats them!"

The old-souls, of course, do not have all the medals. Clearly they have been in the classrooms for a long time and have still not gained release from the need for re-birth. Humility can sometimes be a shield for personal security.

Our Lord made many provocative statements, which although they hurt the hearers were designed to free them from those attachments which called forth His statements in His effort to serve them.

. . . .

Sometimes there comes a cry from some lonely person who seeks their "twin-soul" or "soul-mate." Do these really exist, or is it an optimistic dream that

THE MAN WHO CAN LOOK BACKWARD

things surely must be better than they are to justify being alive? The correct answer really lies within the heart of the seeker. Once they have achieved that inner serenity and peace they do not feel they are missing-out at all. To progress spiritually, we are required to come back into many different physical bodies, some as female, some as male. Sometimes we are happily married, other times we are required to walk alone. This is among the greatest of tests that anyone can be given. But once having passed through the Gateway of Life as an individual our progress is assured. We must learn to be free of all magnetic ties, to relinquish the need to have another shoulder to cry on, save that of the Father.

When tracing-back people's lives I work through their physical name. This makes contact with their spiritual name and it is to this all personal history is attached. On my first visit to the United States I was invited to Hollywood where I gave readings to many. When I asked the ladies for their names, they would give their current name, then their birth-name. "Did you have any other names?" I would ask. "Oh yes, I was originally married to Jim McDonald, then to that rat Jackson," and so it went. Sometimes there were those who had difficulty in remembering their various married-names. This all played a subtle role spiritually. The inner yearning for the ideal conflicting with the restlessness of the immediate present ac-centuates the light and shade of the individual life potential.

As we grow in spiritual understanding we must become less selfish in thought as well as deed, then, in many instances, we find the person to whom w are married can indeed turn out to be our "soul mate." As a camera must be properly focused befor a clear picture can be taken, so with one's outlook and in-look on life.

Links or Attachments From Earlier Lives

So many marriages are unhappy and spent in anguish as a result of discord and I have tried to find out what particular qualities are required to establish that unusual harmony which one finds in some homes. I put the question to a woman, whose early marriage-years were marked with many disputes but who had achieved a wonderfully successful home-life in spite of the disturbing beginning. I asked her to list the five qualites she had found most important for a happy marriage. She considered this for several days and finally admitted she could name only one -- kindness.

. . . .

When people commence to awaken spiritually they find themselves often associated with a group or society interested in esoteric wisdom in some form or another. Strong bonds, or affinities, spring up between members. Provided the sex-force does not rear its ugly head in these friendships -- and we have to remember that we are always attacked through our weaknesses -- then a beautiful and unusual fellowship may develop. This can often last for years or decades. Have these people known one another before in somewhat similar circumstances? It would seem from my reincarnation readings that this is true. The association may not have been particularly close, but links once formed tend to flow back quickly. For some ten thoussand years before Christ there was a wonderful civilization in Egypt with deep overtones of spirituality. The priests and their friends in those days are often re-associated in succeeding lives, if only briefly.

In the same way we may be influenced by familiar forces from the past. We are also bearers of those same faults or weaknesses which may repeat themselves in life after life, until finally mastery is reached and our liberation from that particular stress is ob-

THE MAN WHO CAN LOOK BACKWARD

tained. Because of the variations of our individual backgrounds it is much easier for someone to give up say smoking or alcohol, than another person. Simply, because they have done this sort of thing before and it is easier to do it again. The tie is not so strong.

Frequently at the end of a reincarnation reading the sitter will exclaim, "Why, I'm doing just those same things today. I hadn't realized it before." So, we can be assured that not only does nothing happen by chance, but those difficulties which have beset us in past lives will repeat themselves again and again, in a slightly different guise each time, until finally we have mastered them by making use of our divine will. The emotions or mind may be hurt in the process, but these are healed by the spiritual joy which is our reward.

3

IS IT BENEFICIAL TO KNOW ABOUT YOUR PREVIOUS LIVES?

Like all important and vital questions pertaining to the individual, this one cannot be answered quickly. There are potentials to be considered and perhaps foremost among these is another question: why does one want to know about his past lives? Is he motivated by curiosity? Is there a lurking hope that these past lives were more glamorous, far more so perhaps than the present one? Is it in the wistful hope that in tracing these past lives reason may be indicated for the pattern of today's life?

World teachers such as the Buddha, Jesus, Krishna, Mohammed and many others have come and passed into memory, leaving their basic and similar teachings to mankind, teachings that contain constructive directives to all.

Then why does history constantly repeat itself? Why are there wars - and increasingly horrific and devastating ones, even to the super-bomb threat of destruction of the planet itself? Why are prisons filled and our sick number more than hospitals can hold?

THE MAN WHO CAN LOOK BACKWARD

It is the belief of the writer that an uncreedistic look at reincarnation and a serious understanding of the individualized as well as generalized application of the Karmic law of Cause and Effect, contains the essence of the answer. After all, who makes history - conditions - relations? People. We do. But how are we motivated, by the aggressive and selfish "dog eat dog" method? By the belief that "live-today; tomorrow I'll be dead, that's the end. There isn't any more - just curtains, and an eternal blackout."

In an era that flatters itself that it has evolved an impressive civilization and now reaches to the moon and the planets and onward into the realms of space to the furthest stars, have we learned to live in peace one with the other, person to person, race to race, nation to nation? Surely there is a deep darkness somewhere in the consciousness of mankind that we have not learned how practical the teachings of the Great Ones really are.

"My peace I give unto you," they say to the seeker.

With the understanding of reincarnation comes a realization of the perpetuity of life, of action and reaction, of deeds and consequences, of such sayings as, "We believe that all His sons will one day reach His feet, however far they stray." This is a promise of victory showing that a lost soul is a spiritual impossibility. Fragments of other great truths include:

"Seek and ye shall find - knock and it shall be opened unto you."

"Lo, I am with you always, even unto the end of the world."

"Before Abraham was, I am."

"I and My Father are One."

"What I can do, you can do - and greater."

Eventually, we must all come to realize that God sends his Messengers and their disciples and servers to help us win through to our spiritual adulthood. A

Is It Beneficial to Know About Your Previous Lives?

true believer in reincarnation seeks to understand the inspiring verse in Ephesians 4, wherein the Apostle Paul says:

"Till we all come in the unity of the faith, and of the knowledge of the Son of God, unto a perfect man, unto the measure of the stature of the fullness of Christ,". . . . . . . into the Divine Light, enfolding all.

Our beliefs, however, consciously or otherwise formulated in the shadow of some 2,000 years of physical and spiritual tribulations find it difficult to see any one individual as fundamentally differing from another. They are all spirits in bodies at some stage of the long journey back to God. Each is a bearer of a divine spark which has come into physical form to learn those lessons which only a physical body permits; lessons of association with other persons, with material things such as money, or the lack of it, social standing, the struggle to overcome obstacles and personal situations. Wonderful indeed it is to realize these things for what they are - in the truest cosmic sense - and function accordingly, but we awaken to an interest in more permanent things such as truth, wisdom, love and an understanding as to why we react to those things we gravitate to. As this awareness comes, suddenly we can become free from conditioned thinking which has been imposed upon us by our physical birth, traditions and conditions. We begin to realize there is no real security in any material thing nor in the passing physical life.

Millions of Hindus greet one another by putting their hands together and bowing to each other. It means, "The spirit in me greets the spirit in you." I remember vividly a little English girl in India telling me how Mahatma Ghandi was returning to his home supported by his family after a big rally at which he had been speaking. Although apparently exhausted, he stopped to make this traditional greeting to her - a complete stranger with a white skin.

Obviously there is little opportunity of a mongol child with limited intelligence and probably brief life to grow into "the stature of the fulness of Christ," but if we realize that there is nothing accidental and a very severe lesson is being imposed upon the parents of that child, from which they can either learn or not learn, then the picture begins to make sense - as a whole. A number of world faiths and religious sects, whose followers are leading very disciplined and beautiful lives believe that their particular founder or teacher is a reincarnation of Jesus Christ. Instead of being confused by this claim we can realize that these wonderful adepts and masters have already come into this state of spiritual "fulness of Christ" and their followers are fully justified in their beliefs, justified in a beautiful sense compatible with their spiritual understanding.

I recall a woman telling me how she became an alcoholic. This weakness resulted in her loss of husband, children and home and eventually of all self respect. Picked up drunk on the street, this thirty-five year old secretary was taken to a hospital. During the night she had a strange experience of a man coming to her bedside and repeating to her, "You have one life but many births." When she awoke she was very conscious of these words but she had no idea what they meant. She lived in a predominantly Baptist city and it was not easy to break free from orthodoxy but she tried and on poking around in the public library she came across a book on reincarnation. She read it with hungry absorption. It made a lot of sense to her. It changed her whole outlook, mentally and physically. The truth literally made her free. She started a new career, succeeded in it, returned to her children and together, they lived and fulfilled a worthy life.

Is It Beneficial to Know About Your Previous Lives?

Clearly, one lifetime is not enough to grow into full spiritual stature. Many are needed; in most cases, hundreds. Today, we can speak relatively freely about reincarnation without offending our listeners. But at the beginning of this century we could have been subjected to much criticism and even social ostracism had we brought up the possibility of this truth in a so-called Christian home. Many truths are now open which were closed. Science has opened new doors and philosophers have come forward speaking and writing of the glorious truths of the Ancient Great Ones. Today, millions of English-speaking people freely discuss psychic matters and we are now faced with a new set of questions such as, "Is it right to speak to our dear ones who have passed-on?" or, "Should I know about my past lives?" or, "Can I believe that I will be with. . . . again in another life?"

You can only be the totality of what you have been before and in the same way as many secrets have been prized from the universe in this century, there are many people who believe they have gained much benefit from knowing what they have been before, where they have lived and what are the main reasons for their being in this world now.

As a reincarnation consultant, the reader may say that I am biased. But I am not; I did not ask to be either a psychic healer or to be a reader of past incarnations. Until one of my daughters nearly died as a child I had no wish to be a healer, but after surgery and orthodox medicine had failed to bring any benefit to her I turned to spiritual healing and God touched and awoke my consciousness as a result.

People ask about their past lives for a variety of reasons:
    (1) Curiosity
    (2) Vocational guidance
    (3) Spiritual direction

(4) Present karma
(5) Purpose in life
(6) Marriage

I find, however, that the seeker gets from a reading *no more and no less than his purpose for having the reading.* I would like to underscore that statement.

Is it not the same in all forms of spiritual activity? We have to first give before we can receive. In meditation, prayer or worship we expect nothing back, do we? But it comes, usually in unexpected ways.

As a healer, I have found it very helpful to give a reading for a specific purpose. One of my children, then a 6-year old, was terrified by fire. If there was a gratefire in the room, she would always poke it and try to extinguish it, or put the guard up. If the fire-engine went by she would ask what that noise was, although she knew quite well what it was. Without her knowing, I did a life-tracing for her and found that in a relatively recent life she had been involved in a tragedy in a burning building. Through this reading, we were able to remove the fear and terror she had of fire.

Sir Winston Churchill once stated that, "Only by knowledge of the past can the future be judged."

Recently in New York a man was having a reading of his past-lives. It showed that in his last incarnation he had lived in France and was a physician. After a broken-marriage, he went to pieces and wrecked his life through drink, sex and drugs. The marriage difficulty, however, had been mainly his fault. At the end of the reading, he commented that today he is also a physician and has had the same difficulty with his marriage and similar things which had been his enemies in the past. I am very glad to say there is now in my files a beautiful testimony from this man showing how his life has completely altered for the better.

Is It Beneficial to Know About Your Previous Lives?

Sometimes, I am startled myself as I am shown scenes from the past. A few months ago a very flashily dressed woman sailed into my studio for a reincarnation reading. When I enquired why she wanted the reading, she replied, "I guess I'm curious." I do not do readings for this purpose, so I explained to her that this was not a valid reason for asking to open the records of one's past lives. She changed her reason then to desiring to know more about her present purpose in life. I rather doubted her motives and assured her that if she wanted to find herself as a Cleopatra, or Nefertiti, or the Queen of Sheba she would be disappointed. Nonplussed, she commented, "If you were to tell me I was the Queen of Sheba I would get up and leave the room." Having arrived at some state of neutrality I commenced the life tracings.

The very first life shown was not that of the Queen of Sheba, but it was several thousand years ago in Persia and indeed she had been a queen. She was just as surprised as I was but the reading revealed her as a queen who had been captured by invaders who demanded a huge ransom for her return, ten sacks of golden objects which had been collected from individual persons in the market place.

Sometimes these life-readings are so clear that one can see the exact colors of the clothing worn, of the skin make-up, types of animals, local foliage and architecture. It is fascinating to see the old names of cities and even of streets. Often the former names of the individual lives are also shown. (But to me the most astonishing thing is that I can frequently smell the actual atmosphere. The dank arid coldness of the jungles which house millions of people smells so differently to an Indian market or a Persian bedroom.)

4

WHAT IS THE PURPOSE OF REINCARNATION?

As we look at people we cannot help noticing there are many apparent inequalities of birth. If we contrast the lot of an Australian aborigine with a well-educated American collegiate we must conclude that there is either an unfairness in the distribution of creature-comforts, or there is a definite plan which may not be in evidence to our physical eyesight.

Mother Nature herself is never-ending in her task of supplying man with his needs, whether these be minerals, vegetables, animals or human needs. She is just and fair, having no favorites but allowing man to make use of her offerings as he sees fit. With these he builds and constructs. It is the same with the Divine Will. Each man has been allotted a portion of this great cosmic power with which to determine his own destiny. Nature never excuses ignorance. If a man uses faulty materials in his building, it will collapse. An identical law prevails in a spiritual sense and a

What is the Purpose of Reincarnation?

prime purpose of reincarnation is for man to become familiar with this law. Let us take a few quotations from the Bible.

"In what measure ye mete so shall it be measured to you again." Matt. 7/2

"Be ye therefore perfect, even as your Father which is in heaven is perfect." Matt. 5/45

"Till heaven and earth pass, one jot or one tittle shall in no wise pass from the law, till all be fulfilled." Matt. 5/18

The Apostle Paul, who was himself a lawyer, refers also to this same law of justice in Galatians 6/7: "Be not deceived; God is not mocked: for whatsoever a man soweth, that shall he also reap."

There is nothing accidental in this law, which Paul warns is "not (to be) mocked;" we are on this earth to progress or digress in accordance with our actions and reactions. They are all of lesson, and lessons we have not learned before are assuredly ours again to learn. In school, if we fail to learn and pass our examinations, we must stay in the same class and repeat the lessons until we learn them and pass. So in all phases of earth life.

I have often wondered when looking at an audience, how different they are. Not only do their clothes and looks and ages differ but their backgrounds and foregrounds likewise. Just go back one life in each person. How different again they would be. Some would have yellow or brown skins; maybe some would be crippled, certainly they would be speaking many different tongues, their sexes would be different. Yet each today is the result of his own actions, "I am that I am" expressing on the physical plane. At the center of each soul there dwells God, the source of love and power and the ability to direct the individual in this present and every incarnation.

THE MAN WHO CAN LOOK BACKWARD

Even as we are here to learn not to repeat past mistakes we are also here to undo the suffering caused by our actions in previous lives, sometimes by not repeating those actions which cause pain to others, sometimes by experiencing the pain caused to others.

A dear spiritual healer friend of mine in London, Arthur Kings, printed some cards which he gave to his patients and friends, that quoted a few verses from Psalm 126. Very few of us can fail to perceive the exquisite wisdom in:

> "They that sow in tears shall reap in joy.
> He that goeth forth and weepeth, bearing
> precious seed, shall doubtless come again
> with rejoicing, bringing his sheaves with him."

These words really summarize the law of Karma. It is our divine obligation to progress and this we must whether through sorrows or joys. The immediate decision of choice is always ours. So are the consequences.

Nearly one hundred years ago Sir Edwin Arnold translated the Song of Krishna from the Sanskrit. More generally known as the Bhagavad-Gita, or just the "Gita," it contains the following:

> "No need has he to live that which ye name life.
> That which began in him is finished,
> He has wrought the purpose through
> Of what did make him man.
> No more shall sins stain him
> Nor earthly woes invade his safe eternal peace.
> He lives, yet lives not.
> He has gone into Nirvana,
> Blessed, ceasing to be.
> Om mani padme om*
> The dewdrop slips into the shining sea."

---

*"Hail the jewel within the lotus flower" is one translation of Om Mani Padme Om and it refers to the divine will within the soul of man.

What is the Purpose of Reincarnation?

Saint John expresses a very similar idea in Revelation 3/12:

"Him that overcometh will I make a pillar in
the temple of my God, and he shall go no more
out."

I have met many people who have no wish to come back into incarnation again. Some genuinely mean this; others say it for effect. Only when we have severed our senses from the magnetic attractions which the world provides can we really assert that we do not wish to come back. We must obviously go on living somewhere in some form or another and it is interesting to note that the Psalmist describes man as having been made "a little lower than the angels." An angel has no material possessions but does possess love, wisdom, faith, joy, power and a desire to serve mankind. And this - service and love are the keys to each unlocking the inner door to his true Self.

If we use our spiritual power when we are faced with the problems of life we shall automatically draw closer in consciousness to God until eventually we become immune to suffering as such. We realize that suffering cannot hurt unless we allow it the power to do so. How can we transmute this power? Partly through prayer and study of spiritual teachings and partly through meditation.

Whereas the law of Karma is described as the immutable law, some people ignorantly regard it fatalistically, ignoring the possible consequences of their actions by saying the situation is karmic and therefore "has to be." This they sometimes apply to illness. The truth is that the law of Karma leads, it does not dictate. It is our spiritual will which determines our destiny. When life's problems beset us, it is our responsibility to face them and decide what to do with them.

THE MAN WHO CAN LOOK BACKWARD

I am often confronted with patients who believe they have an illness as a karmic result of some entanglement from an earlier life. Even if this is true, there is still a power the sufferers can use to free themselves from this bondage. This is the power of the Spirit of Christ, of Divine Light, which we have seen from an earlier reference in this book is with us always, provided we use it.

The call of the Christ has always been tremendously strong. A brief outline of how we can recapture this state is through:

   (1) Self-denial
   (2) Self-discipline
   (3) Selflessness.

There is no one pattern of illness from life to life. We are living in a veritable ocean of disease. It is rampant on all sides. We are vulnerable through our weaknesses. If our emotions are disturbed, we are prone to be ill. If we overwork, we open ourselves to a possible mental breakdown. The smoker is prey to lung-cancer, coronary and emphysema-all, killers. No one can truthfully claim it is his karma to smoke. One smokes because that's what he wants to do.

People sometimes say they may never have heard of Christ in a previous life. This of course, may be true. But it is not a physical life of Christ of which I speak but the Spirit, that which is indwelling within all, whatever word be used, whether we are conscious of it or not, regardless of what church, synagogue or mosque one attends. It is not our words or affirmations that matter. It is our actions that reflect our Christ-consciousness:

"As the Father knoweth me, even so know I the Father: and I lay down my life for the sheep. And other sheep I have, which are not of this fold; them

What is the Purpose of Reincarnation?

also I must bring, and they shall hear my voice; and there shall be one fold.... and one shepherd."

John 10.

The purpose of reincarnation is for us to dicover, contact and use our spiritual will in all phases of life. Many of the older souls are incarnating now to help us build a new world based not on the old concepts of divide and conquer, but to share in love those benefits so bountifully provided by God for His children. As Sir Edwin Arnold writes in "The Light of Asia" (translation of the Bhagavad-Gita):

"Such is the law which leads to righteousness
Which none at last can turn aside or stay;
The heart of it is love, the end of it
Is peace and consummation sweet; obey!"

5

HOW IS RE-BIRTH POSSIBLE?

It is important for us to understand that reincarnation does not apply to the physical make-up of our bodies. It concerns only that part of us which is eternal and which on the death of the physical body, is taken into the heavens and becomes associated with our spirit.

The soul is that part of man which can pray and meditate. It is the link between his spirit and his physical mind. When the silver-cord is broken, the spiritual consciousness is freed and the physical body returns to the dust from whence it came. Generally, just prior to this separation, a review of one's whole life occurs in a matter of seconds. The spiritual consciousness then goes to that plane with which it has become familiar during its earth-life. Clearly the plane would differ for a yogi and a criminal. All acts of spiritual merit and demerit are weighed in the balance

How is Re-birth Possible?

by the Lords of Karma before allowing the individual spirit gradually to become re-united with its mother-spirit, from whence it came forth at the beginning of the physical life just completed.

We may liken this process to that of a bulb, which having been in the soil for a season, produces another bulb out of itself. This in turn produces a flower the following spring. At the end of each season the original mother-bulb becomes less obvious but her progeny reflect her reproductivity. In other words, nothing ever dies. Or, as England's former Poet-Laureate Sir Rudyard Kipling wrote: "Come back, come back, for as long as the red earth rolls, God never squandered leaf or tree, why should he squander souls?"

Our mother-spirit bears our spiritual name by which we are known through all eternity. Some people know theirs now; perhaps only in part. Occasionally if a person is sufficiently interested this may be revealed during my readings.

In contrast with this opportunity for the growth of the spiritual part of man we have to take into account the wonderful creation of his body with that part of his mind needed to sustain its growth from conception to the grave. To all this growth the force of instinct and nature's bountiful care must be given correct appreciation. We take into our physical expression those characteristics which have been with our forebears for three and four generations. This means that if our great-great-grandmother had something peculiar in her physical body or make-up, it can manifest in her descendents.

What then of our instincts? What facet of our subconscious mind carries our instinctive reaction to danger, joy, love, disturbances and smells? Do these die with our physical body? If we liken these instinctive reactions to those of our basic animal cravings, we must in fairness assess them as being very similar to those of animals. This is perhaps the greatest truth to indicate how we can - by making use of our spiritual will - awaken the God consciousness within us; this an animal cannot do being unable to reason as man can or should.

A religio-scientific stanza offers vivid insight into the God consciousness, kingdom by kingdom:

God sleeps in minerals,
Dreams in vegetables,
Awakens in animals,
Lives and moves in humans.

Substitute the word "love" for "God" and the picture should become very clear.

Hindu philosophy proclaims:
I died as a mineral and became a plant
I died as a plant and became an animal
I died as an animal and became a human.

These three lines summarize the philosophy of the "transmigration" of souls.

During my readings I spend time usually on the subject's more recent lives that have occurred during approximately the last five or ten thousand years. These have much bearing on his or her present karma. As a rule this is what interests the searcher. Southern Hindus believe we come from and sometimes return to the animal kingdom. Hence, the saying: "Don't kick the cat, you may be kicking your grandmother" has validity to such believers.

The more general belief, however, is that the animals belong in a Group Soul. Those who have lived in close association with humans remain linked with them for quite a long while, still in animal consciousness and form, until returning to the Group. It is thought there is a movement from the Group Soul to the human kingdom at very special periods, such as the beginning of a new epoch. The more evolved animals then enter the human kingdom in the more retarded races.

How is Re-birth Possible?

At what stage of creation does the soul become active in the body of the baby? When does the spiritual growth start in our lives? As soon as the baby "quickens," the wonderful process of uniting the body with the spirit occurs. It is a gradual process, taking the balance of the pregnancy to fulfill the soul-induction, culminating at physical birth.

A friend who is a gynaecologist in London told me of his great pleasure in looking into the eyes of babies after birth. As soon as their eyes begin to focus he could discern the new souls from the old. Some babies' eyes have a look of apprehension and fear; others look around more casually as if appraising their "new" situation. "It was," he commented, " as if they were saying: 'Now what - this time?'."

We are all familiar with the term: "The eyes are the mirror of the soul." This is a true statement as investigation will prove. What is more mysterious is the converse: if there are eyes, is there also a soul? It is quite easy to see from a person's eyes the age of their spirit. This is why when I do postal readings for people I ask for a photograph showing their eyes.

The Lords of Karma are those Spirits who see that there is nothing accidental about a person's birth. Exactly the right karmic conditions are considered which will allow the incoming soul to have the opportunity of progression by using his divine will to overcome those weaknesses and problems that the particular environment will allow. Or, to make amends for difficulties caused in previous lives, and in special instances of merit, to be re-united with one or more loved ones from earlier incarnations.

Everything is part of a great Plan in which everyone has an equal opportunity of "reaching His feet, however far they stray." Nothing is lost. God created everything. Man cannot create. He can only change the form our Creator has given us. When one considers the enormous population of our planet at the present time and bears in mind that most of us have had hundreds of earth lives, one's mind boggles at the task of organizing our karma in exactly the right birth-environment.

Whether the other planets are populated or not, there is said to be a spirit-bank of some three hundred thousand million, so life exists in abundance. It is the precise arrangement of it all that is so fascinating and marvelous.

Readers may wonder where this three hundred thousand figure came from. It is part of the teaching of the world's most authoritative wisdom-school. Today there are many students of astrology throughout the world. And well there may be, as there is so much evidence of similarities with the natures of persons born in related signs. Does this knowledge conflict with the belief in reincarnation or karma? No, it does not when one bears in mind that we are not dealing with that part of man which will return to the earth at death. The characteristics evident from astrological charts refer - in most cases - to his mind and physical features which generally fashion his nature and make-up. We are dealing with his eternal spirit only, and while the physical vehicle for that spirit may be influenced by the stars, there are certain solar energies, or rays of which and by which his soul is composed. This has been described as a diastolic and systolic action of the divine ethers.

Even as the soul commences to form in the new baby at approximately three to four months, certain energies must be used to allow this spiritual link to form. There are seven distinct energies of which the soul is a combination, having one energy - or ray, as it is more generally termed - uppermost, or apparent.

This is why an individual is sometimes described as being a "First-Ray" person. As with astrology,

How is Re-birth Possible?

karma, atomic secrets, heat, light and sound as well as matters connected with mind and spirit, a fuller understanding of this esoteric knowledge is more possible today than it has been for centuries. Man today has made many esoteric truths common knowledge and is thirsting for more. The old souls now incarnating are determined to make this world a better place to live in and there will be much greater emphasis in the future on establishing truth in connection with spiritual matters and less on the false security of dogmatic "truth" or possession of physical things, which in themselves have no permanency.

A proper study of the rays is of interest to truth seekers. It is fairly easy to determine those born predominantly on one of the seven different rays. Alice Bailey, through whom the spirit of "The Tibetan" wrote at great length, has written several thousand pages on this subject called "A Treatise on the Seven Rays." Ernest Wood and Geoffrey Hodson have added very valuable contributions on the subject, thus making a rich knowledge available to seekers.

It is beyond the scope of this small book to go into the different features of the various rays. This is a study in itself requiring more than a casual interest to be of value to the seeker, but it is noticeable that most people connected with the theatre are "on" the fourth ray.

This particular ray, being in the center of the seven, expresses the other six in quite a dramatic manner. An actor can usually, at will, assume various characteristics and thus portray other people. It is difficult for a fourth-ray person to find "himself." It is far easier for him to be someone else. His karma therefore is rather more trying than others of the rays until he makes greater use of his own spiritual will, and less of his ability to mimic. I remember Peter Sellers, an excellent character-actor, saying how for years he lived "like Cary Grant," conducting himself in his relationships and generally behaving as he thought his model did. It was very difficult, he admits, for him to find his real self.

Each ray has a particular color, distinct from the auric color. It encircles the head and connects with a spot close to the heart, rather like an egg in shape. As a person's spiritual devleopment unfolds, so too, does this ray-color change in size and acquire a golden fringe indicative of his spiritual quality.

If you wish to further study the rays, I recommend a splendid little book by Mr. Geoffrey Hodson, "The Seven Human Temperaments," obtainable from any Theosophical Society.

6

VERIFIABLE EVIDENCE OF FORMER EARTH-LIVES

Having been brought up in the school of hard-knocks I have never taken kindly to those speakers who preface any remark which is at all out of the ordinary by: "It is said." As a truth-seeker I have always looked for evidence which can stand up to any investigation. Although I knew in theory that spiritual healing was possible, I did not know how to use this universal power until I had seen it at work in bringing my very sick daughter back to health.

When we start to investigate "these things" we become aware that there are two distinct types of persons making public appearances, writing books and so on. There are the quoters and the knowers. I have never favored the former type of evidence. I like facts. . . . just the facts. A fact is something which has happened. It is prudent never to reject anything when hearing it for the first time, however unusual it may seem. A wise way is to defer judgment until further evidence

THE MAN WHO CAN LOOK BACKWARD

is forthcoming. Merely to quote someone else, who may also be quoting, is unfactual and confusing. This particularly applies if you are asked a question which requires a direct answer.

We have all heard people say, "I don't believe in reincarnation" or rather arrogantly say, "I don't buy that." To deny what they know little or nothing about merely proves they have closed their minds to the possibility of its truth. Far better to wait for further evidence before committing yourself one way or the other.

Books have been written on reincarnation which quote, as a case in point, stories from the lives of East Indian children. Many such stories offer very strong evidence of children who have been able to name people and places thousands of miles from where they live. Associations which it would have been impossible for them to have made during their present lifetimes.

Personally, I have never liked the evidence of children. There are other explanations which could validate their undoubtedly true statements. Before one starts teaching publicly on a subject as "way-out" as rebirth it is usual for strong evidence to have occurred to convince the person of the reality of this subject. Otherwise the proof is second-hand.

In my own case, I had listened to many lectures on the subject but I still was undecided; I neither believed nor disbelieved. I just did not know. Then three evidential things occurred. They took place in 1958 and in one form or another all involved the remarkable psychic quality of L. T. Symons, who at that time was living in New Zealand and who had been the healer involved in bringing back normal health to my daughter after a long and distressing illness.

It was a Sunday in October; I had been giving spiritual healing treatment to Frank....., a Czechoslovakian mystic with unusual abilities. After he heard my prayer for his recovery, he thanked me and I answered impulsively, "It isn't the first time we have prayed together." There was a strong recognition of being together before and I had a shadowy picture of where and the circumstances, but not knowing him too well and being rather uncertain about what I couldn't prove, I discontinued the conversation. That evening we both attended a meditation group for the first time together. At the end of the evening the man mentioned earlier, Les Symons, came over to Frank and myself. I introduced them and the conversation went like this:

"Well, Frank, you and Noel should get on well together."

"Oh, yes," replied the Czech in his broken English, "We do."

"I don't mean just as you are now," said Les Symons, "I mean as you were when you lived in France and were an army commander. I don't see you with Noel today. I see him as he was then - a priest and he was negotiating with you about ending a war. I see you then wearing a helmet. . . ." He never finished the sentence as Frank interrupted him saying:

"Oh yes, I know that story - my helmet had horns in the front and I wore a breast-plate of armour. I had lace-up boots and carried a small sword."

My own recollection was rather hazier than this, but I did know of this earlier incarnation as a priest - quite a few details of it, in fact. I also just an hour or so earlier had experienced the odd feeling of having been with Frank spiritually at some other time.

This evidence was not sufficiently strong to do more than stimulate my interest but it did confirm that two strangers could have known of this same earlier existence of one of them, in which I had apparently featured.

THE MAN WHO CAN LOOK BACKWARD

On the Wednesday of the same week a young chap in his early twenties, Peter ... from London, had dropped in at dinner time. He was a well-educated young man who was at that time touring with a theatrical company and doing any sort of odd job that was offered him. He would probably be called a drifter today. A nice fellow but always short of money; hence his visit. Les Symons had also come in for dinner and we had talked of various things during the meal. We three were sitting in the lounge when Les asked this younger chap if it was true to say he had been interested in the study of ancient civilizations. We had not mentioned anything of the sort and these two were strangers. Peter replied:

"Well, if by ancient civilizations you are referring to one particular civilization, then you are right."

"It is the Inca civilization, isn't it?" asked Les.

"Yes, it is." How did you know?" said the young actor.

"Well, when you came into the room to dine with us, you sat opposite me and I saw the fourth order of priesthood over your head in the Inca civilization. As I was also a priest in the Inca period I was naturally interested to see if you had any recollection of this incarnation."

"Well, I'll be blowed," was all Peter could say. This was something he had not learned at the university, but to show how God moves in mysterious ways and at the least expected times, the following conversation ensued:

Les Symons said: "You see, life is not all spivving round here and there and getting yourself engaged every few months. If you wish to really get down to some hard work you can again use your wisdom and do some good for other people."

That ended the conversation. We broke up soon afterwards and I was left with yet another interesting

Verifiable Evidence of Your Former Earth-Lives

experience which really did not culminate until some five or six years later when Peter rang me up in Sydney, Australia to ask me to have coffee with him. He looked very smart and sophisticated. He had seen in the papers that I was lecturing in this city so he came along to tell me he had taken notice of what Les Symons had told him and had almost immediately commenced studying to be a psychiatrist. He was now working with children and enjoying it thoroughly.

Later that same week I was talking with Les about a man who kept a metaphysical bookshop in New Zealand. I enquired if he knew him. He replied in the negative but just closed his eyes, and on picking up a carpenter's pencil which was lying nearby on a table, drew some symbols on a piece of scrap paper. "Next time you see him, ask him if he knows what this is," said Symons. I went into the shop the following day and picked up a book I wanted. Seeing the owner I spoke to him for a few moments and taking the piece of paper from my pocket I asked him if this particular sign meant anything to him.

He turned rather pale and enquired who had given it to me. I said who it was and he commented he did not know him, but the sign was in fact the ensigna of the order of monks he had been in in Italy in his last life. He went on to speak about his life then as if recounting a dream.

That was my reincarnation week. I did nothing more about it until I had become a full-time practicing healer and was sitting with the patient in London who, as I mentioned in the first chapter of this book, was unable to go out by herself. From that time onwards there were frequent pieces of evidence indicating recognition from people who were having readings. Among these was Sarah, an elderly white-haired spiritual teacher from Wellington in New Zealand.

In one of her past lives I had just been shown her

as a girl living in Canaan some fifteen hundred years before Christ, when suddenly she burst out singing a song which she declared she had sung during that life. "I have known about this life," she exclaimed with joy at the verification.

During public demonstrations of tracing-back lives I am sometimes at a loss to describe happenings which are distressing to the listener. Remember, this is to a complete stranger who has volunteered to have this tracing done. It is always the same at public meetings. After I have traced back the lives of some of the persons present, they all want it done, so I usually ask suddenly, "Would anybody like their lives traced back?" I take the first few hands I see raised, asking the persons chosen to write down their names on a piece of paper. In 1960 I was demonstrating at the Spiritualist Association of Great Britain in 33 Belgrave Square in London when I saw in a past life scenes of the French Revolution through the eyes of one of the onlookers who was alive at that particularly distressing time in France. I could not do more than say to her that she had lived in France and a few nebulous things such as liking animals and so forth.

The next day she telephoned me to ask if what I could not describe at the meeting had anything to do with her hating violence in this life and also having a strong dislike for knitting. It was this last question which surprised me, for as students of French history will know, during the actual time when the noblemen and women were being beheaded by the guillotine these scenes were witnessed by delighted spectators called the "knitting women" who would knit into their woolen garments the names of the persons being beheaded before their eyes. It apparently gave them great pleasure.

I have received hundreds of testimonials in my work as a spiritual healer and in connection with my re-

Verifiable Evidence of Your Former Earth-Lives

incarnation readings. At first I thought very highly of each one and wanted to frame them! However, there was one which I have good reason to remember as it occurred soon after I had started doing these readings by post. The man was from Liverpool. He had written down some of his past-life "flashes," as memory-incidents are called. During one of his lives he had recorded that he was of French birth and lived during the 18th century. He had written that he played a spinet.

Imagine his surprise when he received my reading to find these details verified even to the extent of my writing that he "played a spinet." He was very pleased at this confirmation.

Today people who come for readings often comment: "I can feel myself in all of these lives." One woman commented that while the reading was going on, she felt a strange activity at the back of her head. Others have said they have felt a tingling in their spine.

As a researcher, I am always on the look-out for evidence which is substantial. One day a master of a school for boys came to see me with some photographs of an old house in England where he wished to move his school. He said he felt strangely attached to it when he had viewed it on several occasions. Spreading out the photographs on my desk, I went into the Silence for him. The old house was originally built rather differently with a wing at the side which had been dismantled, but I could see this schoolmaster in the 17th century visiting his mother in this old wing. He was then a physician. I was describing the scene of how he was returning to his coach when two dogs bounded out to greet him. "Oh yes," I heard him exclaim. My conscious mind fastened on to this like a flash, so I wrote down the type of dogs I had seen. "Can you see those dogs?" I enquired. "Oh yes," he said. "What breed are they?" I asked. "I don't know the name of the breed," he replied, "but they are tall dogs with curly tails and pointed faces. They walk with very springy steps." I then handed him the piece of paper on which I had written the name of the type of dogs I had seen. "Afghan hounds," he read aloud. "Yes, that's right, that's what they were."

. . . .

In my records I have a signed copy of the following happening in India. It is reproduced here without comment.

THE BOY WHO FOUND AND LOST HIS "WIFE"
..... as told to Noel Street by S.M. Sofaer.

"These events took place in 1930 in Calcutta where I was living. I was fourteen years old at the time. It was just before seven o'clock one morning when I arrived at the small baker's shop in Elliott Street where each morning regularly I fetched fresh hot bread, straight from the oven for breakfast.

There was a crowd of people gathered round the shop. I managed to get near enough to see a small boy, barely twelve years old, talking to the woman who usually served me. I would say she was then in her late thirties.

She was terribly agitated, for the boy was trying to convince her that he was her deceased husband. Fantastic though it seemed, he was reminding her of when they were married, the house and the village they lived in and the family they raised. He went on to relate personal and intimate details of their married life, which no one but her own husband could have known. I do not know how this reunion ended, as I had to be back home to get to school in time. Needless to say I was not served any bread that morning.

The baker's shop remained closed for several days

afterwards and when it reopened it had a new face and new people working it. From rumors I heard, the woman had returned to her native village."

7

MAN'S IMMORTAL HERITAGE

Longevity has always been sought by man. Many are the reputed means of gaining this extension of life. At the beginning of World War II, when I had become unwillingly caught-up in the military bulldozer, which lasted six long years - I was struck by the absurdity of man's adroitness in supplicating God to justify killing his brother man.

All religions are explicit that man is a divinely-made being and we are told not to kill one another. In 1941 I was lying in a military hospital with a leg injury. In the morning the radio broadcast a thrilling message by Sir Winston Churchill which concluded with the fitting rhetoric to justify his call for further efforts and that Hitler would be defeated because, "The mills of God grind slowly, but they grind exceeding small."

In the afternoon the radio also broadcast a speech by Adolph Hitler which referred to the fact that

Germany's right was a divine right and therefore she would march to glory. What about the young soldier lying in a hospital bed? The kiss of death, or the wine of life? I wondered as I wrote these lines:

> Jester immortal - harlequin of fate
> Who knows no time, no bonds, no space.
> Star of stars, life's emperor of hate
> Laughs, and beckons to our maddened race.

I did not then know the reality of reincarnation but I did think about it in a strange way. My elderly mother - bless her - had been born in a medical specialist's home in London in Wimpole Steet. Her father had been a brilliant physician. At the birth of my older sister, the nurse in attendance, who had known my grandfather, had remarked to my mother, "What a beautiful girl. I wonder if she has the soul of your dear father." My mother was aghast at this idea but when she told me the story, it stayed in my mind. It was the first reference I had ever heard to reincarnation. Can you remember when you first heard of this belief? Try to remember.

There are very few truths which make such an impact on a person's psyche as reincarnation. It has been described as an immortal mirror.

Its reflections can adjust, disturb, consolidate, reveal and often attract with glue-like magnetism as some happening from long-ago comes back to today's consciousness.

As with the story of Peter in the preceding chapter, a person's life can be altered in a twinkling-of-an-eye. Such an incident was reported in THE EVENING NEWS, Newark, New Jersey, Dec. 6th, 1968 under the heading:

"PSYCHIC TRACES REINCARNATION"

" 'She's an interesting girl,' said Rev. Noel Street, a psychic healer from New Zealand, as he scanned the face of the youngest member of his audience at Friends Meeting House, 289 Park St., Montclair, N.J. last night.

" 'She was an Indian female on this continent in the 15th Century,' he said of his 12 year-old subject. 'Artistic, good with colors, pottery, skins. She had healing skills, too, and an excitement about life. The older she got, the more pleasure she got out of life.

" 'But an experience with her husband - she had many suitors - set up a Karmic condition, which relates to her health in this lifetime, but I can't discuss that in an open meeting.'

"The psychic, who avers that many life conditions such as illness, emotional instability and unhappiness have their foundations in previous incarnations, closed his eyes for a minute or so before continuing.

" 'I see her again in Holland in the 18th Century. This was a more stable life, less freedom. She didn't like the discipline of her home. She escaped its restrictions by an early marriage. But marriage wasn't too happy for her, reinforcing the Karmic condition.

'VERY SPIRITUAL GIRL'

" 'She had an agile and alert mind, absorbed knowledge easily. In her later life associations with people furnished her with great vitality. Very spiritual girl,' he concluded.

"Mr. Street, a tall broad-shouldered man, whose facial features would suggest a prize-fighter were it not for a gentle expression, said that people's past incarnations unroll before his mind's eye as if on a screen. All he needs to get the multiple biographies under way is the subject's name.

"He said such ability is latent in everyone. 'Lots of people have had flashes of earlier lives, recognizing places they've lived in before, people they've known before. But they are not conditioned to pursue such inklings, so their immediate impulse is to disavow them.'

" 'Take a book one has read a long while ago and doesn't even remember having read. Then a character comes to mind, then another, then a scene, and as soon as one starts to read the book again the entire story comes to mind.' "

. . . .

The girl who was sitting with her mother at the meeting was a complete stranger to me and the block which I had seen concerning a male influence was too intimate to describe in public. I was glad, therefore, when the mother visited me privately for advice on this point. An almost identical Karmic pattern had set up in this present life. It related to a domestic situation, which the mother was most happy to recognize and adjust.

It seems that man deliberately, in life after life, involves himself in situations which can only cause sorrow, until at long last he uses his spiritual will to avoid being entrapped in unfortunate situations.

A life-time in relation to eternity is but as a twinkling-of-an-eye. Suppose you are intent to get to a certain place in a hurry. You are travelling on foot and have already successfully negotiated several streams by adroit skipping from rock to rock. Now, faced with a larger river you use the same tactics and are drowned. To you, it has meant several days travel and finally death, without having achieved your journey's end.

Now let us look down at the same scene from a point high above the earth. What took several days and covered maybe many miles, would appear to be an almost imperceptible speck moving across land divided by thin threads of water. The obstinate traveler, instead of crossing where the river is shallow, blindly pursues his pathway until destroyed by his own limited geographical knowledge of the terrain.

When man regains his inner powers he will know the right way. And in this manner he will not repeat his mistakes, for once overcome, that particular problem will not trouble him again. Instead he will have others to learn. For each lesson learned, however, there is a chalice of joy (which far exceeds the momentary pleasure or success gained through selfishness.)

A very strange reaction came from a person in Nottingham, England. In my reading to him I had found him caught in his last two lives with a very difficult sex-problem. It was far from straight-forward. He wrote that he was trapped with the same difficulty in this present life. He not only wrote about it in some detail, but there were sixty-four pages of his innermost thoughts poured out to me. I recall putting the letter aside until the end of the day when my family were going to the movies. I started reading it directly they left and was still at it when they came back. Every page was vitally important to him and as a result of the reading he had received he was able to meet and finally conquer this recurring concern in his life.

Each faces his own individual problems. Each battles for release from them and victory always brings greater strength, greater understanding and greater joy.

One of the most interesting things about reincarnation is that there are no exceptions to its rule. We may think we are not important enough to be of much concern in the heavens. But we are, the Divinity that does not overlook the sparrow certainly heeds His children.

For most readers of this book, I am sure, life in abundance lies ahead in their incarnation. For others, ideas and truths developed in this lifetime may well be world-wide beliefs by the time they incarnate again, so the activities and spiritual progress of each form the whole now to fashion the world-pattern of tomorrow. We have only to look back say, a mere fifty years to see how the pattern of spiritual truth has altered. There is a wonderful spirit of freedom available now - perhaps as never before - illustrating the working-out of the Great Plan on earth as we move away from the emotional age of Pisces to that of Aquarius, or the age of knowledge.

There are today in this country over forty colleges and universities teaching Para-Psychology. This is a medium of knowledge that brings quiet understanding and subdues the emotional aspect of religion. It is likely that the structures of today's emotional forms of worship will give way to identifiable evidence of man's one-ness with Spirit. Herein lies love, truth, security, unity and brotherhood unseparated by dogma or "spiritual brain-washing." Many gods, once deified and worshipped by followers now branded as "pagan," have already become lost in the unending maze of history. Many others, now popular, are liable to join those whose heads have already rolled in the churches of yesteryear. Why? Because they required their followers to have too much blind-faith and not enough truth. As the wise Mahatma Ghandi once said, "All gods are good and all men are brothers."

Men, in the form of priests, have never had much difficulty in creating "gods." Rarer indeed, is the gift of being able to awaken the psychic powers of the worshippers, so they too can see and commune with these gods.

It is easier for the man-in-the-street to grasp the idea of a form of a god than being taught how to become familiar with the spirit world. Hence this latter has for countless centuries been regarded as dangerous.

THE MAN WHO CAN LOOK BACKWARD

Yet, the Apostle Paul is emphatic that the discernment of spirits is a spiritual gift.

Who is wrong - the Apostle or the priest? The danger lies in the manner in which the discernment is carried out BECAUSE VERY FEW PEOPLE ARE EVER TAUGHT THE WAY.

. . . .

When we find something good which is evidential we like to share it with our friends, do we not? Man is by nature generous and kind, so in presenting the following extracts from letters which people have written to me after either visiting me for personal consultations or receiving postal readings of their past earth-lives, I would like you to see if you can pick the "golden thread" which runs through them all. Note the global interest, yet similarity of expression:

(1) *From New Zealand* "Thank you very much for your letter and survey of past lives. It was very interesting and true. It was very helpful and certainly strengthens my belief in reincarnation and our purpose here to overcome our present state. Those characteristics are still with me, so no wonder I'm here!"

(2) *Los Angeles, California* "Almost a year ago I received your life reading which I found very interesting. Since then I have read a lot of books and any kind of literature which referred to reincarnation. I came to understand much more the great work you are doing and the help and understanding of themselves you are able to give others."

(3) *Perth, Australia* "I must thank you for the most enlightening reincarnation report. I am most grateful, for it has helped me greatly. So much has been

Man's Immortal Heritage

explained. For instance you told me that 'my emotional drive was so disturbing to myself and others that I was my own enemy.' Well, unfortunately that is still the case, but I mean to drive it out in this incarnation or bust!"

(4) *Wellington, New Zealand* "I just want to take this opportunity at Christmas time to thank you again and let you know of the great benefit I have had from the reincarnation readings. So many things connected with this present incarnation had puzzled me and now it is all so clear. I can see the past and present woven together in a tapestry and all related in a way I could not do before, even though I had studied reincarnation. The way ahead is clear and I feel the readings have been a milestone in my spiritual progress."

(5) *Rochester, New York* "Thank you very much for the three fine readings you made for me recently. I could not help but think as I read them that in each one there was something, emotion or trait, incident or circumstance, which appeared to be identical with my present life. Again I wish to thank you, but in reality I cannot thank you enough."

(6) *Brussels, Belgium* "Many thanks for your kind letter. It is amazing to see how my present self seems to emerge from the various pieces. I showed the reading to a very old and close friend who easily recognized me in it. You have a wonderful gift."

(7) *Denver, Colorado* "Thank you so much for your letter giving me the reincarnation reading which I found most interesting. You said in my former lives I had studied mathematics and astronomy. Well, apparently I haven't changed any, since I am by profession an actuary with an insurance company and my chief hobby is amateur astro-

THE MAN WHO CAN LOOK BACKWARD

nomy. Thank you again for all your help."

(8) *South Devon, England* "All the things which I have done in the past lives you outline still appeal to me, so now I understand why they do. I am glad that our spiritual powers, when once awakened, are ours for ever. Shall go on endeavoring to improve the present."

(9) *County Armagh, Ireland* "Thank you for your reading of some of my past lives which I received recently. I can trace all the influences you refer to, in my present incarnation."

(10) *Uralla, Australia* "Thank you for my reincarnation readings. You certainly picked "me", better than some people who have known me all my life. I have all those qualities you refer to in my readings."

(11) *Cape Town, S. Africa* "Your reading of my past lives, which arrived on Christmas Eve, was the most wonderful Christmas present I have ever received. You are quite right regarding the negative qualities in my past lives, because they are still my weaknesses in this life, but now I have the courage to try to overcome them with God's help. I wish to thank you for a most accurate and fascinating revelation of my past."

(12) *London, England* "I already see a link, or thread connecting ALL the incarnations you have mentioned and coming out in the present 20th Century life."

(13) *Aberystwyth, Wales* "The readings have definitely helped me to realize what a lot of conflicting emotions there are in my make-up. So many of these feelings I used to push to one side but now realize that it was foolish as they really were the real "me," so perhaps now I can tie these threads a little more together."

(14) *Reykjavik, Iceland* "I thank you very much for your kind letter which has certainly been of much help and interest to me. My intuition tells me that you are stating facts in your letter and I am thankful that a world-famous healer like you, gives himself time to answer my letters personally.

(15) *New York, U.S.A.* "Thank you very much for your very helpful report. My husband and I were very much impressed with his former incarnations as they seem to bring out the high points of his character in this life. He is a lawyer who has worked very hard and is successful. He often wanted to be a teacher."

. . . .

These are just some of many testimonials which are in my files, yet we find mirrored in them man's ability to see not only the good and the flattering, but those negative traits which block the positive and prevent the God-within from shining forth in complete radiance. The expressed desire to cope with imperfections, however, is indicative of the growth into conscious spirituality.

8

HOW YOUR LIFE CAN AFFECT THE WHOLE WORLD

Many scientists today believe that man's ancestors originally stemmed from the amoeba, or simplest form of microscopic animal-life, evolving over vast aeons of time during many changes on the earth's surface to the upright two-legged creature he is today. This may well be true. There are other theories of course, but it would seem fairly evidential that man as we know him today is a very different being than he was thousands of years ago before he started to make use of fire.

He appears to have become spirit-conscious soon after this as there is evidence that he commenced not only to bury his dead but through fire cremate the physical body. In this act, he differed from the animals; probably because he was able to be in touch with the spirits of those who had passed-on, so out of respect they were given burial by one of the elements.

How Your Life Can Affect the Whole World

When our parents were children the family Bible was as much the center of the home as the television set is today. From this Holy book, wisdom was served in liberal doses. So liberal indeed that many sickened of the fearful fate said to be in store for us all. This is so recent that it must be taken into account in its relationship to the many churches we have today, most of which have been functioning as edifices of worship and truth for hundreds of years. These family Bibles listed in chronological order the happenings in the Old Testament, commencing with the Adam-and-Eve account of creation. This is listed at four thousand years before Christ. Yes, 4,000 B.C. Look for yourself. This "truth" satisfied former generations. They either did not like to question a book regarded as being inspired by God, or feared to question it.

During the last two to three billion years many forms of life, both plant and animal, have inhabited the earth and then become extinct. The main way we know about them is through the study of fossils. Recently a necklace of fossil seashells was found with the skeleton of a woman who died 30,000 years ago.

It is interesting when looking backwards along people's life-tracks to find them in civilizations which are now extinct. Some have crumbled into the dust of deserts, some lie on ocean bottoms, others have vast jungles growing over their temples. Some are rediscovered. In Indonesia I recently saw a Buddhist temple containing over a thousand life-size statues of the Buddha. It was described as having been built over a thousand years ago "by unknown hands."

No doubt many of us are familiar with the old civilizations of Atlantis and Lemuria, or at least familiar with the terms. Some people will delight in telling you they were "on Atlantis." It appeals to their romantic vanity because secretly they think they were kings or queens, or at least high-priests or priestesses.

THE MAN WHO CAN LOOK BACKWARD

No lowly social level for these dreamers. It is good to have an assortment of ideas reflecting in different people. It makes the world interesting and colorful. This is one of the oddities of reincarnation. Until a person has studied it for a while, they find the idea magnetic and attractive, mainly because they hold to a fond hope that at one time they were vastly more important than they are today. Some women delight in thinking they were "lovers in ancient Egypt" with some present heart-throb. Popular "IWASES" are Cleopatra, Pharoah (any one will do), Nefertiti, Marie Antoinette, Mary or one of the disciples.

Certainly, one of the currently popular views held by reincarnationists is that we continue on to other planets. This seems probable and one meets people today who claim to have come from other planets to this one. There is not enough real evidence to support this fully, at present; but there probably will be in the immediate future as our spacemen look beyond the moon and the planets of our solar system to the far solar bodies in space.

One of the most wonderful mysteries which is now no longer a secret is our knowledge that man is a pilgrim-god who can by making use of his God-like powers gain access to the kingdom of heaven. When man establishes for himself that love is a reality and not just a selfish experience, he will be able to use that power of love to alter not only his own life, but those around him.

If he is in business, his whole outlook changes. He continues to prosper but enjoys his life more. If a housewife discovers this secret, her nature completely changes. She has become aware of the beauty of things around her. If a man is crippled and unable to leave his room without aid when he discovers love he is released from all suffering attendant with his physical limitations.

How Your Life Can Affect the Whole World

How then can this mystery be discovered? To know God is to know truth. "Ye shall know the truth, and the truth shall make you free." Some people expect life to be a continual donor. They become frustrated when other members of their family or social group acquire perhaps a new car or added professional and social position. God is life and God is love. People are prone not to give first. Too often they give in a calculating way. This is how trade is conducted. It is not how the heavens are organized and "run." No spirit there possesses anything except love and those virtues which go with this, foremost among which is service, one to the other.

When one discovers reincarnation one sees life as a continuous flowing stream in which we have the opportunity of making our present life one of supreme achievement. We no longer see anything as permanent and cease to strive for personal ends. We start to give more, until finally this becomes part of our nature, although we may not know this for certain: the more we give the more we will receive. This is the test of our sincerity. No words can do this. It requires action, but as we realize we are giving to another person .... who is also the bearer of a divine spirit, another pilgrim-god in fact, we find to our amazement that we are really only giving to ourselves. "I and My Father" and I and my Brother are ONE.

Our consciousness has become enlarged and we can appreciate how we are in touch with the entire world through the spirit of love. Man has been described as the microcosm or as a lesser world of the macrocosm, the universe or greater world. The powers of God in all their universal greatness are reproduced in man in miniature.

This today is one of our greatest tests. Although continents and races are much closer than fifty years ago, there is still a long way to go before we realize spiritual unity. We still think in terms of how is it going to affect us and we are still bound by our environmental localities, rather than being able to exchange in love our thoughts and difficulties that we may be able to examine them together in the light of God's love.

This is why so many wonderful "old souls" are coming back today into incarnation. Man has now mastered the ability to destroy on the greatest scale in the world's history and if it were not for the wisdom of the more advanced thinkers he would have done irreparable damage to our earth and the elements. In fact, he may still do this. The "younger souls" would stop at nothing to achieve their goals of power and conquest.

However, if the Apostle Paul is right in his statement: Eph. 4/13

> "Till we all come in the unity of the faith, and of the knowledge of the Son of God, unto a perfect man, unto the measure of the stature of the fulness of Christ."

then we can realize that we are living at a most momentous time in the history of mankind on this planet, as we are coming closer to the period when we shall be able to "all come in the unity of the faith" when such universal powers of God as love, faith, spirit, worship and truth are able to be used for peace and progress for all mankind.

The action must come from each individual. Each is the lesser world which affects the whole. "By their fruits ye shall know them" and this is a law of all Nature, inclusive of man.

An American poetess Angela Morgan wrote in a few lines what is in fact the substance of these last pages. The poem was termed "Passports". It runs:

How Your Life Can Affect the Whole World

"Hurl then thy cry at Heaven's gate;
God will admit thee, soon or late.
Thy passport? Saints could ask no more,
God's image at thy very core."

So that you do not put down this book in disappointment thinking that it may be right, but what can you do about it; I will hasten to tell you that in the next chapter but one, there is a very simple way of doing something about it - constructively. I have found a great craving in the world for more knowledge of a subject which is universally spoken-of but very little practiced.

It is yet another jewel from India's diadem and may well become the next major interest in man's spiritual life.

We have in this century discovered how through radio sound can be conveyed from one place to another. This was seemingly miraculous but when it had reached its zenith we were then shown how light as well as sound could be conveyed from scene to scene. Then followed colored light. What next?

Yet another hidden truth has already commenced being extracted from the universe and man has already begun to experience the exquisite joy of being able to gain for himself direct truth. At present this is not general knowledge but it is in fact, the main reason why you are reading this book. Imagine being able to tune-in with your mind to a source of wisdom which can instruct you on such fascinating subjects as reincarnation, karma, meditation, the spirit-worlds, man's inner powers and finding that there is a secret language by which you can unlock inner truths.

When you are able to accomplish this relatively easy process you will realize more fully who you are and why you are here today.

. . . .

THE MAN WHO CAN LOOK BACKWARD

Some people are so interested in their past incarnations that they will have several visits or readings, possibly in connection with one particular life, which may be of especial value. One such was Alan, a pilot from London. He was exceptionally anxious to know if he had been alive at the time of Christ so I agreed to try to find out. He was well-balanced emotionally and spiritually so such information would not confuse or disturb him, one way or the other. When in the Silence I could see him in another male body actually witnessing the crucifixion. During this remarkable re-enactment of history the spectators were forced from the actual spot where the crosses stood to a slope some fifty yards away. They were kept back by strands of rope held by Roman soldiers. Just prior to the Spirit of Jesus leaving His body, the vibration of this happening was so great that the onlookers fell to their knees bowing their heads to the ground.

When the reading was over, I was most interested to know that this friend's teacher had told him persons who witnessed the crucifixion "had a certain mark on their foreheads." He was told he too had such a mark. He did not know its relationship to his bowing to the ground as he shared, in some measure, the supreme sacrifice being enacted and which his eyes, out of adoration desired not to see.

9

SPIRITUAL VISIBILITY IS BECOMING CLEARER

We are just on the threshold of seeing yet another prophecy fulfilled. It concerns what has been described as "man's last enemy." We are told that we shall be able to overcome death. Just as the inner and hidden secrets of the universe are today excitingly being discovered and put to use by man, so too we are within touching distance of what will be man's greatest achievement.

For long stretches of life-times man has been in fear of death. He has been promised so many dreadful happenings when he dies that few, if any, have looked forward to the quite natural passing into spirit-life. This has been caused by his spiritual education, or diseducation, preventing him from realizing that we cannot die, however much we try, and also believing that God should be "feared," rather than loved.

Some years ago, while visiting in the Solomon Islands, a native asked me, "Why did God make man?" After giving a few semi-convincing reasons for creation, I asked him what he thought. A grin stretched across his shining black face as he said, "God wanted us to love Him." If we relate this simple explanation to man's struggle today to build more and more concrete jungles, to enforce illegal acts towards a neighbor's country by superior ability to kill him or exploiting and even annihilating the animals for our own ends, we can realize that we are not yet to be trusted with the keys which unlock the door of "man's last enemy," but we are on the very verge of it.

As we learn to love God more and to serve Him by serving our brother man, we shall also learn there is no such thing as death. Death of the physical body is associated with fear, rather than a release of an old garment no longer required, that the spirit may return to its source in the same rhythm of love in which it has been accustomed to live. A continuous river of life and love, halted for stops only, during the whole of which time our purpose is the individual realization of the God within each and every man.

Death and life are one. Most of us are aware that we can still be in touch with our loved ones, who have passed into spirit life. Some of us can do this ourselves, others consult psychics trained to use this gift of bridging the two worlds. A dear old friend of mine, whose psychic powers were made use of by the British Navy during the last world war, was happily married for many years. His wife passed on some ten years prior to his own journey home. She had always had a great sense of humor, which he, in turn responded to with hearty booming laughter. After his wife passed on, he sat with several mediums to reach to and speak with her, but unfortunately he had to discontinue this as she was always so pleased to be with him that she would make the same kind of jokes as she had in life and this would cause his hearty

Spiritual Visibility Becoming Clearer

laughter to wake up the mediums from their trances! Now, however this dear couple are together again in spirit.

Today many books are published on the revival of the old gift of prophecy, whereby man can see into the future, a future that can be verified. So much then for the present as it relates to the future by way of the invisible worlds, but what of the past in its relationship to the present?

We have now established without fear that man can still be in touch with spirit. Many people have been persecuted, tortured and killed for their gifts in this field. Would it not be of great help to know more about the past of an incoming soul? Is this not again one of the doors which is slowly being forced open by man's enquiring into reincarnation? We have proof of the continuity of life; why not the beginning? Everything in nature is continuous and rhythmic. In this century there have been some fine books written on the topic of re-birth quoting various types of cases of "recalls." I have tried in this humble little book to show how knowledge of the past can help the present as very often we bring forward obstructions from earlier happenings which can be removed, provided they are recognized.

Often we are not conscious of these blocks. For some obscure reason we do not feel clear in certain directions. In my own life, I have never liked the sea. As a boy of eight I never read sea-stories. I wanted to be among the trees, in the forests with the animals and birds. I would get up at 4 o'clock in the morning and go for long walks. It was not until many years later that I learned that I had lived as a North American Indian.

An American woman was with her husband and friends in a museum just outside Mexico City. The tour of the old Aztec section was being conducted by a guide; as she listened to his explanation of the various artifacts of this vanished civilization, she immediately developed a dreadful headache. While he was speaking of the different relics, she knew it was wrong. Something within her was telling her the correct roles which these articles played in the lives of the Aztec people. She became so disturbed that she went back to her hotel. She made a point, however, of seeking the guide to query the source of his information. He admitted it was mostly his own beliefs and had little historical background to support it. She wrote me this story at length. It is in my files.

I have found this type of memory-recall fairly common and could cite many similar instances. They are termed "flashes." Often that is all they ever are, but should the person receiving them become reoriented with the same locale in which these old memories were birthed, then the flash becomes enlarged into a very vivid scene. Generally these flashes have no location or time, but it is astonishing how many people have found them to be like an electric-light switch which on being switched on by returning - (of course accidentally, as they don't know for certain where they occurred) - to the same spot, a long forgotten memory from a bygone life revitalizes with remarkable clarity. Should any readers have had this experience, the writer would appreciate hearing from them. Also, if you can relate this to the lives of any animals.

As there are now so many human recalls and so much evidence of past-lives on earth, it would be of great interest if we could establish the same evolutionary process in animals. I have often asked this at public lectures for listeners to send me verifiable cases of animals which have had obvious recalls of past lives. I have collected a few such instances, but would like more before putting them into publication.

The bridge forward into spirit has been established. We are now constructing the bridge backwards. When this has occurred we shall see our present life of supreme value to both, for it indicates exactly where "we" are now. The past is memory oft-forgot; the future but a dream. But the will of the individual is for the present and all the tomorrows.

We are looking for world-brotherhood, unity of worship and the ability to use our God-like powers. As love is the key to these divine quests what stands in the way of it being more fully utilized?

Satan was walking along the road with a friend. He was overtaken by another man who rapidly passed them. Suddenly espying a piece of paper on the ground, he picked it up, read it and commenced to dance a little jig in the road. Grinning broadly, he put the piece of paper in his pocket and hurried on.

"What's he found?" enquired the friend to Satan.

Being clairvoyant, Satan replied, "He has found a piece of truth."

"Huh, has he now?" said the friend, "That's bad business for you, isn't it?"

"Oh no," said Satan, "give him time, let him organize it, then he'll lose it!"

Christ could walk on water. I have seen Fijians, even young children, walk on white hot stones with their bare feet. I have also heard ministers of religion, whose beliefs are said to espouse the former as miraculous, condemn the latter as being "Satanic." Needless to say, the ministers themselves could do neither.

Fear and ignorance in spiritual matters is lessening. In a fuller sense it has deadened man to his God for centuries, but now the world is becoming so much smaller mankind is again realizing we are all one-spirit at different stages of the journey home, to our return to full-spiritual awareness.

Before we pass on to the chapter, which concerns

THE MAN WHO CAN LOOK BACKWARD

how we can gain entry into the inner-worlds, let us briefly say it is through our desires we can make use of our will-power, either to digress or progress. Our desires influence our thoughts. As Professor Huston-Smith of Mass. University wrote:

"Sow a thought, reap an act.
Sow an act, reap a habit.
Sow a habit, reap a character.
Sow a character, reap a destiny.
Sow a destiny, reap a God."

10

THE KEY TO YOUR SPIRITUAL TREASURE HOUSE

To be even partially successful in gaining and using your spiritual knowledge, it is essential that your motive be to draw closer in consciousness to your God-mind. You will be shown here the keys which will open the library doors but you will never be permitted to use them unless your purpose is rooted in love, unselfishness and service. The man known as Jesus had all powers. He was as God. "I and my Father are one."

He also said: "What I can do, you can do, and greater." By virtue of the Divine spirit within us, we can merge in this consciousness. We can contact teachers on the inner planes who are able to impart knowledge to us which will enable us to progress into a closer likeness of our God Master.

Prove this for yourself. One way is through Meditation. Meditation requires practice. It is not necessary

THE MAN WHO CAN LOOK BACKWARD

to go into retreats in places of solitude. God is everywhere. We are part of Him. The way I have demonstrated on television and on radio has been described as the most effective and beautiful form of meditation yet revealed to man. It is so simple, yet it took years to be unveiled to me in a usable form. It is based on the belief that God is approachable through light.

In this procedure we break up light into its component colors:

Red		Blue
Orange	Green	Indigo
Yellow		Violet

We then take this "light" from the lowest vibratory rate into our consciousness by concentrating on it in a certain manner. Then we go through each of the remaining colors. It is a way of drawing one's consciousness closer to God as light. Also the converse applies; we can draw light closer to our mind. It permits our consciousness to separate itself from the emotions, the physical body and the mind. We thus become very similar to spirit.

Whilst it is not suggested that this way is better than other methods of meditation, it is effective as it does not disturb any type of psychic or other development being undertaken. In fact, it is complementary to anything of a spiritual nature. It is also absolutely safe. For nearly ten years now I have taught this in many countries and places. It has been used by church groups and other teachers. I am only too glad, as all truth must be shared and no strings attached. Ultimately, when this way has permitted the seeker to gain direct truth for himself, it will not be needed as there is no necessity for any "method" as such, to reach into spiritual consciousness.

At this stage, however, it is emphasized as there are relatively few people who can gain direct truth, although many who can meditate. We can liken this way to steps which eventually can be dispensed with through practice.

Meditation, to be beneficial, must be done regularly to awaken and strengthen the inner powers. It is preferable to meditate at the same time and in the same place. The best time is as close to dawn as possible. The worst time is late at night. It is advisable to keep a notebook and pencil handy, both during the period of meditation and while asleep, for once having commenced to open the door of the mysteries, the inner sight opens. If we record what we "see," this enlarges and other parts relative to it will continue to enlarge and enrich.

Regarding dreams, dreams which are in color are directly from spirit. Often just before going to sleep, we may be shown faces of people we do not know, places we have never been to. These are recalls from earlier lives and are indicative that we have begun to tap the sources of truth. Let it be emphasized that these are just preliminary manifestations, exercises if you like, to condition us to the normally unseen worlds.

It is interesting how similar things, which seem so wonderful when they happen to us as individuals, occur to many people at this same stage of understanding. Either in groups or as individuals telling me of their experiences, they well say, "I saw an eye" or "I can see an eye." Often this is said with such surprise. But it is all quite normal. It indicates the seeker is awakening his third-eye, which is the eye of the soul. But this cannot be done without making contact with some other power external to himself.

. . . .

Let us assume the preceding conditions can be complied with and the student is sitting quietly in a

THE MAN WHO CAN LOOK BACKWARD

chair with spine erect, clothing comfortable and in a harmonious atmosphere. A little music or incense helps to prepare the right "temple" in which to worship. If you practice yoga, the lotus posture is ideal for meditation.

Thoughts are things - we can visualize anything we wish. Energy follows thought.

So let us create with our consciousness a temple in which we are about to worship. To enter our temple, which may resemble a cathedral, a mosque or just a small chapel, according to our visualization, we have first to mount seven steps to reach the doorway.

The first step is colored RED. On this we stand, and in so doing, feel the vitality of that beautiful color emanating like a cloud enfolding us. We pause for a moment to fill our mind with this power before moving on.

The second step, which is ORANGE in color now welcomes us. It is like stepping from one cloud into another. We stand enfolded by this lovely radiance for a few moments until proceeding upwards to:

The third step, which is like a mighty sunbeam, YELLOW in color. This warms us as it enfolds us in its beauty and power. After becoming enclosed by this we proceed to:

The fourth step, which is colored GREEN. As we pause, we become identified with this harmonious life-giving color. It is like being a flower feeling the security of green garments, except this is spacious and inspiring. It has been rather like walking into a rainbow. We proceed now to the next step:

Which is pale BLUE and is not unlike walking into a cloud. We feel cleansed and uplifted in this lovely color. We pause for a few moments.

Passing upwards, the next step is INDIGO or dark-blue. It vibrates peace and power as if we are approaching a sacred place. In deep reverence we proceed to the next and final step -

Which is colored VIOLET. It is peculiarly soft and loving, yet strong and compelling. We have now reached the door of the temple. What lies beyond?

Our door opens. We are drawn inside, still conscious of having passed through the veils of color and light. We are attracted to an altar before which we kneel. On top of the altar, shaped in a semi-circle, are the same series of seven colors: Red, orange, yellow, in the center is green shading into the pale blue, dark blue or indigo and violet.

It might be best to make a drawing of the order of these colors. They never vary in nature. Every rainbow or dewdrop is the same. Even on the inner planes, they are in this same relationship, but vary in intensity. Make sure you know the right order, first for the steps, then the altar. If you meditate as a group, one of you should guide the others verbally.

When you first start this practice you will notice some of the colors are more intense than the others. You may not be able to "see" any of them to begin with, but after a few days you will find they will come into a lovely flowing pattern. No two people see them exactly alike. They may be dark or light. They can vary as much as our karma does. However, we have to remember they are only steps to discipline our mind into a controlled state so we can reach beyond it into our spiritual consciousness.

When we have completed both sets of colors we now employ our will again to uplift our minds to that which is most sacred to us. Most of us may term ourselves "Christians," or, as I do, "Free-thinkers," but we have a profound humility and awareness of the Christ-love and Christ, of course, is LIGHT. To be Christed is to merge in THE LIGHT. Now with our consciousness raised through this battery of colors, all of which are shining brightly, we place a cross in the center of them. The cross is a Divine, not a creedistic symbol, although it may be both. Concentrate on the cross. You may see this as being of gold, or light itself, or white. Whatever it is, use the very utmost of your will-power to retain it.

This is where the battle starts. Your mind will wander off into all sorts of byways. Don't let it. Draw it back to the cross, until you finally feel at one with the spirit lying beyond that emblem. Allow the Christ-love within you to flow to the Spirit of your Lord and Master. In so doing you will clear the way for a wonderfully close understanding between the spirit-world and your own consciousness.

This way of entry into the Silence is equally powerful, no matter what your religion, or if you have no professed religious beliefs at all. Simply concentrate on that symbol of the highest form of spiritual love which you know and revere.

As a few days will elapse before you can be certain that you are "in touch" so to speak, persevere. Do not try this form of meditation more than twice a day. Once is generally sufficient. Initially, do not stay in the Silence for longer than fifteen to twenty minutes. It is quite in order to do this with friends. If you know how to chant the aums, or a friend can, this will add to the effectiveness. Just as you move from one color to another, aum can be quietly chanted, either by one person, or preferably the whole group. The emphasis should be on quietness with no one voice being noticeable.

Do not alter your normal spiritual habits because you are meditating, or have just discovered reincarnation. Continue to worship in the church of your choice. Everything should be added to spiritual growth, not something taken on as something else is discarded.

We must give first before we receive. However, it is advisable every night unfailingly to ask for protection before you go to sleep, both for yourself and your loved ones. A simple prayer along the lines of: "May the Guardian Angels of the Christ Light watch over... ..... (then list the names of the persons concerned, terminating with your own) tonight while we sleep.

This state of spiritual growth is clearly stated by the Blessed One in John 16/13:

"Howbeit, when he, the Spirit of truth, is come, he will guide you unto all truth; for he will not speak of himself; but whatsoever he shall hear, that shall he speak and he will show you things to come."

Our whole growth, both in this present incarnation and those past, is similar to that of a flower. There is first the parental growth, then the gradual development of the forthcoming progeny - through bud-stage to final flowering glory - then the gradual return to the soil, to re-appear once again with the same life-force within but a slightly different outer cover.

. . . .

Even as our soul-ray is the uppermost color of those light-forces used in fashioning us, by using this form of meditation we can enlarge our light-field and become conscious in higher forms of life.

After a short while, we will be further instructed in a manner which it is not wise to indicate in a book, so this can really only be like a ticket for a train ride.

The ticket is light.

In Australia the aborigine says he is "lighting" something. This means he is looking for or finding something which is invisible. He is contacting its vibrations.

11

CONCLUSION

Mindful of man's eternal quest for inward, as well as outward, peace; aware of his innermost desires to achieve success and gain full heritage in his every field of interest, John Whittier wrote his well-known hymn, "Dear Lord and Father of Mankind," which includes this verse:

"Drop Thy still dews of quietness
Till all our strivings cease;
Take from our souls the strain and stress
And let our ordered lives confess
The beauty of Thy peace."

Very few lives really know this inner beauty and peace. The stronger the stress upon the outer, upon the material world, the further the inner reality recedes from consciousness. The more weary the stress and tension of the outer life, the more remote the inner strength and calm. We become as an unprotected body beaten by mental and spiritual travail. When the suf-

Conclusion

fering is too intense we cry opprobriums upon the God that has deserted us. The darkness closes in tightly, the night swallows us.

Nothing, however, happens by chance. As it has been, so it will be; as it is, so it once was. We make the pattern. We mold our destiny, great, small, indifferent or blank. The creative forces ignored by us in thought and deed, or activated by us in thought and deed, set or do not set reaction into motion. "An eye for an eye and a tooth for a tooth" is not a mere biblical bromide. It is a stern religio-scientific truth. It is the backlash of thought and deed with which we draw to ourselves creative forces that shape our ends. When these ends appear just that, our despair cries out against the unjust God who may note the sparrow's fall but ignores our own.

But our emotions and prejudices notwithstanding, the Higher Law is just. It is simpler, however, to accept it when life moves pleasantly.

It usually mitigates our difficulties when they arrive by blessing them. The simple phrase: "Thank you Father" is most efficacious when said as a prayer, either when joy or sorrow strikes us. The pain becomes eased as we realize we are growing in wisdom through our suffering.

We can learn many of the deeper truths through an understanding of how the trained athlete functions. He meets every test. He may not always be victorious but he follows through. We might emulate this spirit in our life and follow through, for even as we make the effort and do so, as a challenging phrase I once heard in Australia describes it: "Nothing is so permanent as change." Already, there is change. A new vista. New challenges. Therefore cleave to the Wheel of Life, revolve in harmony with Nature and the Higher Spheres. Soar in consciousness. Meditate. Awaken inwardly and contact the God-mind, the Reality within. Progress into the inner peace, strength and serenity that belongs to you. Only the illusion of the material world separates each from his own, "I Am the Resurrection." It is true. Each is. We die. We are born. We die. We are born. "Nothing is so permanent as change" - on and on and on. Citizens of Eternity moving ever onward, slowly or rapidly, but always progressing to the ultimate realization, "I and the Father are One."

St. Paul states: "I die daily." This speaks of the physical death. Death is birth, birth is death. They are the Black and the White of the same Image, back to back. They mark our coming and going. Incarnation after incarnation, until our eyes pierce the veil and we stand forth in Soul-Spirit reality, a shining Wayfarer merging with the God consciousness.

Whether our life pattern be easy or hard, joyous or sorrowful, it is what we have made it, either in godly or godless moments.

It is not the purpose of this book deliberately or by innuendo to convert anyone to a particular faith. To each his own. All paths eventually lead HOME. How long it takes to reach this ultimate destination is our individual problem, our individual challenge. But our completed Book of Life has a happy ending. Reincarnation teaches us that a lost soul is a spiritual impossibility. All must return to the Godhead from whence all came untold aeons ago.

James Marlow, an Irish poet, writes a somewhat whimsical interpretation of this:

"On a rusty iron throne
Past the furthest star in space
I saw Satan sit alone.
Old and haggard was his face,
For his work was done and
He rested in eternity.

Conclusion

> Then to him from out of the sun
> Came his father and his friend,
> Saying: "Now the work is done
> Enmity is at an end."
> And he guided Satan to
> Paradises that he knew.
>
> Raphael came winging down
> Gabriel without a spear
> Uriel without a frown;
> Welcoming their ancient peer.
> And they seated him beside
> One who had been crucified.

This may seem irreligious, but is it? Was it not necessary for Judas Iscariot to incarnate or for Satan to fall from his once-exalted position in the heavens in order to allow God's plan to manifest for mankind?

Belief in re-birth in no way alters our spiritual way of life; it does however offer a more rational explanation of some of the apparent anomalies of creation than is normally taught in our churches. We can understand that a retarded child is not a reflection of an angry Diety, but an occurrence completely in accord with certain laws that must be fulfilled. Drunken husbands or wives, difficult marriages, child-prodigies, unexplained feelings towards people and places and many other imponderables have now taken on a logical and just purpose, as a result of which the persons concerned can either learn the required lesson, or have to come back into yet another human body to be given the same task all over again.

If there was a library available on the most remote island on this planet which contained records of everyone's previous lives, their present karma and purpose for being alive now, there would be many pilgrims to its doors.

Yet such a library does exist and its membership

is open to all who are prepared to qualify. You will remember the true story earlier recounted in this book of the owner of the bookshop in Auckland, New Zealand to whom I showed a roughly drawn insigna which he immediately recognized as his priestly-order in his last life. It was drawn by a person who had never seen him and did not know him, yet obviously the knowledge had come from some "library" of which these two men - complete strangers to one another - were familiar.

If you would like to be able to read "the records" yourself, the ability is very close to you - it is just your will away. Christ is very explicit on this point in saying "the very hairs of your head are all numbered" and in the same chapter (10) in Matthew this verse: "For there is nothing covered, that shall not be revealed; and hid that shall not be known."

It is my belief that today man is tearing aside the veils of many mysteries and matters once thought sacrilegious for the layman to know, such as prophecy, discernment of spirits, the gift of healing and the tremendous scientific changes we are experiencing, all adds up to the profound truth that we are miniature-gods struggling to return to our full stature and just beginning to take advantage of our wonderful heritage, mentally, spiritually and - to some extent - physically.

The direction is in accordance with our will uniting with Thy Will as purposefully we tread the Pathway - now being cleared of shadows and rubble, the Pathway of Reincarnation, until at long last we understand, we know and we become the LIVING REALITY of: I AM THAT I AM.

>Happy traveling, Brother Man - Citizen of Eternity, Pilgrim-God.

- The beginning -